ALL ENTANGLED

Poems

Ann Floreen Niedringhaus
ANN FLOREEN NIEDRINGHAUS

WISE INK

ALL ENTANGLED © copyright 2021 by Ann Niedringhaus. All rights reserved. No part of this book may be reproduced in any form whatsoever, by photography or xerography or by any other means, by broadcast or transmission, by translation into any kind of language, nor by recording electronically or otherwise, without permission in writing from the author, except by a reviewer, who may quote brief passages in critical articles or reviews.

ISBN 13: 978-1-63489-413-5

Library of Congress Catalog Number has been applied for.
Printed in the United States of America
First Printing: 2021

25 24 23 22 21   5 4 3 2 1

Cover design by Nupoor Gordon
Interior design by Patrick Maloney

Wise Ink Creative Publishing
807 Broadway St NE
Suite 46
Minneapolis, MN, 55413

Distributed by
Spring Hollow Books
6908 Wentworth Ave. S.
Minneapolis, MN 55423
612-232-4096
Available at Amazon.com and select bookstores
For quantity pricing, write us at springhollowbooks@gmail.com

Only . . . poets are unafraid of ambiguity; everyone else goes to experts.

    —Edwin Friedman

The gift of a lifetime is to be the same person

    in as many places as possible.

        —Sarah Bellamy

CONTENTS

Acknowledgments · 7
Street-Side Basement Window · 11
1953 · 12
Words · 14
Safety · 15
Survival · 16
Vigils · 17
Emerging · 18
Paying Attention · 19
The Cycle · 21
Family Picture, 1917 · 25
Clothesline Reveries · 26
From an Airplane · 27
From the Interstate · 28
Friendship · 29
Heini's Stories · 30
My Mother's Story · 31
Mom's Summer Peaches · 32
Your Mother's Home (Namibia, Africa) · 33
Time · 34
Lately I've Been Losing Jewelry · 35
El Salvador Visit, 1987 · 39
Chicago Back Porch, 1951 · 40
On My Way to Art Class at Age 9 · 41
Early Marriage—West Virginia, 1968 · 42
Teenaged Girl · 44
Daughters with Disabilities · 45
That Day · 46
After First Diagnosis · 47
Anxiety · 48
Rider · 49
Mayo Consultation · 50
Swimming Lesson · 51

In the Beginning · 55
Onions · 56
Marriage · 57
All Entangled · 59
Release · 60
Equipment · 61
Finding Equilibrium · 62
Hope · 63
1982 · 64
Motherhood · 65
When Rachel Turned Forty · 66
Still · 67
Long After the Funeral · 71
Mount St. Helens · 72
Your Voice · 73
During War in Afghanistan · 74
The Zoo · 75
My Work · 76
Certainty · 77
In Praise of Fog · 78
Aging · 81
The Old Woman · 83
Her Photo · 84
Quilts · 85
One Word · 86
If I Lose My Memory · 87
This Face · 88
At the Funeral · 89
The Past · 90
Autumn Garden · 91
Rainy Morning · 95
That Moment · 96
To My Adult Daughter · 97
Clues · 98
Lighting Candles on All Saints' Day · 99
Unexpected Wonder · 100
Life Forms · 101
Morning Glories · 102
Happiness · 103

About the Author · 107

ACKNOWLEDGMENTS

With profound gratitude to:

Robert, for his love and empowering support
Rachel and Beth, for ALL they are, for all they've taught us
Deborah Cooper, Candace Ginsberg, Ellie Schoenfeld, and Anne Simpson, for wise guidance and good humor along the way
Alyssa Bluhm and Patrick Maloney from Wise Ink and cover designer Nupoor Gordon for essential, supportive, high-quality skills and guidance
Brad Thompson for his distribution and marketing assistance

And with thanks to the following journals and anthologies in which the poems below first appeared, some in a previous version:

Albatross: Autumn Garden, Morning Glories, That Moment
Art Word Quarterly: From an Airplane
Bearings Online: Anxiety, Lighting Candles on All Saints' Day
Bellowing Ark: Unexpected Wonder
Calyx: Vigils
Coe Review: Aging
Common Ground Review: 1953
Convergence: All Entangled
Crone: Emerging, The Old Woman, When You Turned Forty
Fox Cry Review: Heini's Stories
Good Courage: Marriage
Loonfeather: Family Picture, 1917
North Coast Review: Street-Side Basement Window
Peregrine: The Cycle
Plainsongs: Clothesline Reveries (chosen as a Plainsongs Award Poem)
Rattle: Happiness
Reader Weekly: Emerging
Sidewalks: The Widow (now At the Funeral)
Sojourners: My Work
The Comstock Review: Swimming Lesson
The Ekphrastic Review: On My Way to Children's Art Class

The Teacher's Voice: Teenaged Girl
The Wolfhead Quarterly: Survival

BOUND TOGETHER: LIKE THE GRASSES (Clover Valley Press): Friendship, Hope, My Mother's Story, Paying Attention

THE COUNTRY DOCTOR REVISITED (Kent University Press): Early Marriage—West Virginia

THE MOON ROLLS OUT OF OUR MOUTHS (Calyx Press): During War, Lately I've Been Losing Jewelry, Life Forms, Motherhood

RESPONSE (Calyx Press): In Praise of Fog

WRITERS READ: VOLUME I (Little Big Bay LLC): From the Interstate, Your Voice

The following poems appeared previously in the poet's chapbooks:

LIFE SUSPENDED (Poetry Harbor, 2003): Daughters with Disabilities, Family Picture, 1917, Mount St. Helens, One Word, Safety, Your Mother's Home

PARALLEL TO THE HORIZON (Pudding House, 2007): Below, Marriage, Still, We Could Be (now Finding Equilibrium), Word

. . . what is obscure but ready to be significant.

   —William Stafford

STREET-SIDE BASEMENT WINDOW

There is nothing forcing me
to stay here; and yet
I stand on tiptoe for hours
following the parade of passing feet,
feeling within me, even when I turn away
the rhythm I cannot hear.

Patterns change throughout the day:
drowsy beginnings,
midday rush, weary returns.
I need no clock.

One day I walk out
and join the flow of moving bodies. At first
I can only look groundward.
When I finally look up,
there is no danger, there is no hope:
no one meets my eyes.

I turn around
and descend the steps again.

Some feet, their pace, their tread, are
recognizable no matter what they wear.
I've learned to watch for them
and be reassured.

1953

I admit it. I never said anything—not to
my hovering parents, not to anyone ever—
how I walked alone
in dappled shade along the vast park
across the street from my home, walked
down the sidewalk, blocks away from
our solid brick house, walked
toward the New Jersey Palisades
where I could study mist inhabited by
Manhattan's buoyant gray spires
floating above fog-bound river.

I must have been ten, at most eleven.
We left there, North Bergen,
before junior high.

Never a beautiful child,
photos of the time record
my prominent teeth, bright eyes, open face.

Across a grassy median, his car
was parked at the curb, door open.
He sat on the passenger side facing me.
His car formed a metal barricade between me
and close-spaced, work-emptied buildings
with steep front steps. And he spoke—
Look what I've got. I still remember
his exact words. Obedient child,
my feet started me in his direction.

Then, mid-course, a torrent of
mother's words, repeated often,
drenched me:
Avoid strangers.
Be careful when you're alone.

Go with your gut.
I veered sharply, walked firmly, resumed
my path away from home
to that beckoning horizon.

WORDS

Linguists claim that words are what make it possible for us to think.
I struggle when I try to put my feelings into words.

We first wondered if our daughter had a disability
when she continued to use single words instead of moving on to sentences.

I'm not convinced that words are an advantage for us.
Child therapist Annie Rogers states we discover loss as we acquire language.

It's probably no coincidence that humans start to develop speech
just about the time they learn to creep away from their mothers.

The moment I name something
I diminish it.

When my clergyman Father's mind was failing, the gibberish of his monologue
was rich with words like "justification" and "hermeneutics."

Trying to capture mystery, John wrote in his Gospel,
The Word became flesh and dwelt among us.

Our daughter is more sensitive to people's facial expressions than to what
they say. Her first reaction is to wonder if they are watching and judging her.

I've never been able to whistle, roll my *r*'s, or curl my tongue.
When I was a child I doubted I was a competent person.

Dr. Keith Moore finds newborns are attracted to and distinguish between faces.
He hopes he has provided evidence that humans think before they have words.

Annie Rogers's second book describes *the hidden language of trauma*.
She chose for its title: THE UNSAYABLE.

SAFETY

Okaukuejo Waterhole,
Etosha Pan Game Park, Namibia

In night spotlights, you, giraffe,
      come to the waterhole to drink,
stand motionless, except
your tiny head turns slowly
watching and listening.

Your vigil lasts a long hour,
the same minute motions
repeated again and again.
When at last you fold to drink,
your legs, straight and widely placed,
form a stiff sawhorse.

There's always a lion
at the Okaukuejo Waterhole.
Today I saw her smeared red,
eating springbok.

How do you know it's finally safe
to bend down to drink,
to expose your vulnerable neck?

SURVIVAL

The peacock knows
how
to strut
and fan his tail
so
no one asks for anything more.

After all
with so much loving detail:
    the iridescent green,
    the vibrant blue;

why would you look beyond?

VIGILS

The second robin stands on the driveway
as I open the automatic garage door.
I raise a curtain on her vigil. I failed
to figure out how the first robin died yesterday
in my garage. I simply found him there
and dumped him unceremoniously
into the gray plastic trash can by the door.

Now the second robin—unmoving, unstartled—
stands guard. She has fixed her gaze
on the inside of the garage. She looks
through me to the place where she must have
last seen her mate. And I wait,
unable to drive away, forced to watch her
and think my troubled, admiring thoughts.

EMERGING

The sprout pushes up
cockscrew bent,

draws power
from shrunken bulbs
newly plumped
by rainwater in subsoil,

forces excess
through striated walls
    into leaves
    and tendrils
    and buds,

breaks earth
into chunks,

reaches for light
dimly seen
at the last moment.

Then blinded
as the final membrane
is breached,

its push
is doubled by pull
    of light
    and warmth
    and admiration.

PAYING ATTENTION

Carefully I glaze a clay pot. Will I recognize
which one is mine after it's fired?

Early in her dementia my mother was frustrated by
what she could not recognize. Later she didn't notice.

Denise Levertov wrote, . . . *sometimes I am*
hidden from the mountain in veils of inattention.

All rock and soil in the earth's crust
together make up less than 1% of the globe's volume.

I am naturally ambitious and impatient. I have
much to learn from my daughters who have disabilities.

―

Sometimes I feel like people in many traditional cultures do:
it can be threatening to be observed.

Franz Wright said, . . . *everything seen*
is something seen for the last time . . .

Gradually my daughters learned
to ignore people who stare at them.

The ordinary consoles me. It gives me
visceral knowledge that this has happened before.

Robert Creeley said he learned more about writing poems
from raising chickens than from any university professor.

―

In his novel, Hesse quotes Siddhartha:
The opposite of every truth is just as true.

My daughters are more capable
of appreciating mystery than I am.

To be absolutely certain in our opinions, we must
ignore the size of the universe, the complexity of a cell.

Sometimes, in sunlight,
I am able to see the iridescence of dust motes.

After a long hiatus, the hibiscus
gathers up its juices, spits forth a scarlet bud.

THE CYCLE

Insight begins
with a flicker in
    the corner
    of my eye.

Once I'm
snowed in,
    forced to live
    a human pace,

exhilaration
collides with
    visceral
    limits

until meaning
is constrained
    within bounds
    of words:

those simplifications
restricted
    to what
    I can speak.

Gradually
words shrink tight
    around
    my throat,

till unprepared
I glimpse again
    peripheral
    flutter.

People are

more than their current selves.

—William Stafford

FAMILY PICTURE, 1917

Grandpa was a pioneer pastor—
   served parishes in Bovey, Minnesota;
   Poplar, Wisconsin; Bradshaw, Nebraska;
   Haxtun, Colorado; Cheyenne, Wyoming—
   always moving on.

Grandma followed her husband,
   saw her son suffer rickets and leg braces,
   shut herself up in asthma attacks,
   died young of heart failure;
while Grandma's brother logged out Port Wing, Wisconsin,
   filled ships bound for Chicago,
   clothed children in fur-trimmed coats,
   photographing them for posterity.

Grandma's memories went back to Sweden where
   sons preached in the same cathedral for 200 years;
   but in America, clergy were not aristocracy.
For all Grandpa's learning and elocution,
   he was a country pastor in a land
   that prized board feet and young skyscrapers.

In my album Grandma's disappointment
   lies registered on her pale prim face.

CLOTHESLINE REVERIES

Sometimes I'm my mother
leaning out our apartment window
drawing toward me, hand over hand,
the pulley-threaded line anchored into
sooty bricks next to a window jamb.
I send each dress and shirt
off toward the far matching wall.
Methodically I assemble a parade
of colorful banners, brash signals
above the heads of occupants below.

Sometimes I'm Henry Niedringhaus
planted in my perfectly mowed back yard
where wind whips through, snapping
wash smartly. Baskets brim
with laundry from seven. My ropey arms
reach and lift. Their muscles remember
three days of work: swinging a lantern
to signal the engineer, grabbing an iron bar
to pull myself aboard the rolling train.
I hang skirts, trousers, underwear, socks as
each family face passes before me. Neighbors
may call me henpecked, but I don't care.

And sometimes I'm the Grandma Larson
I barely knew, hanging up clothes
alongside a red-painted farmhouse. I take my time
in brief respite from stoking flames
in the radiant wood stove, catch
light breezes in damp Nebraska heat.
Menfolk can wait in their nearby cornfield,
yearn for steamy black coffee, unadorned
bologna sandwiches. Faded work clothes
hang limp around me—hide me, give me cover.

FROM AN AIRPLANE

Like a night-flying insect hovering
over the flower earth,
I scan a circuit board of lights,
straining to see
the cluster for one small farm
in glow of yard lights.

I imagine a young man coming in
from the barn, deciding
his life is too small for him,
while I envy how self-contained
it all appears. It seems the center
of a panorama, a twinkling oasis
pulling me. Probably he imagines me
unfettered. I could tell him
I'm imprisoned in this fuselage.

FROM THE INTERSTATE

Deserted, early morning. A new house
rears up through spring leafing trees.
Raw lumber plastic-wrapped in nursery blue
rends their lime-tinted mist.

In high grass at grove's edge where
prairie encroaches, a ghost farmer
dithers and searches, seeks in vain
the ancient barn long rising from this plot.

Over and over I've noted this mile point
never even slowing—
hailed the barn's stately timbers
growing from fieldstone foundation. I never
stopped to walk the hill
shadowed by that towering frame, never
stroked those paint-free boards
worn silvery smooth, nor
pounded them to test how solidly they stood.
Not as he did.

This day again I glance away,
let the next curve carry me out of sight.

FRIENDSHIP

> ... for Robert

Each South Dakota summer
in the upstairs boys' bedroom
the Fourth of July rodeo
would come to him through the screened window.

Waves of words, backstopped by broader roar
of crowd response, lit in his brain
flashes of the hump-backed Brahman bull charging
a prancing clown, a wiry cowboy perched on
the hoof-launched bronco.

                     So when he heard
his friend describe a Brooklyn balcony
off Bedford Avenue near Ebbets Field, where cheers
for the Dodgers rose and fell, where random words
pierced distant din giving clues to how the day
would end   the South Dakotan recognized
the sense of boyhood and of longing that they shared.

HEINI'S STORIES

1. The one about the cook
at the Beanery in Marmarth, North Dakota,
where railroad men laid over between trips.
She used to fry their breakfast bacon in lard.

2. The one about the blizzard,
when the "rails" spent the night in a hotel without
much heat. Another "rail" came in covered with snow
and someone asked, *What room did you stay in?*

3. The one about barber Roy, who
once asked Heini how he wanted his hair cut.
Heini said, *What difference does it make? You always
cut it just the way you like it anyway.*

4. The one about the time at the Mobridge Depot
when one rail told the others about cutting off a finger
in his car's fan. With his car hood up he demonstrated
how the accident happened and cut off a second finger.

5. The one about Heini bargaining for a used car
with his favorite dealer. After a tough interchange
Heini said, *Reuben, the only difference between you
and Jesse James is you don't wear guns.*

Once there was a German immigrant named Henry
who signed up as a brakeman with the Milwaukee Road
in the 1940s. He'd come through Ellis Island when he
was fourteen, five years after the First World War ended.

He worked off his passage on an Iowa farm, at a
brickyard, and in a meatpacking plant. He labored to lose
his German accent. He was a rail for thirty years and
honed his stories right through the Second World War.

MY MOTHER'S STORY

She told the story at some point in every trip we took—her surefire way to keep our interest and pass the time. How they met at fourteen and seventeen, she the older. He, the pastor's son, unnoticed, smitten by her lively, slightly naughty demeanor. How he carried his silent crush through his family's frequent moves; till, at last, from Cheyenne, a thousand or more miles away, at least ten years later, he decided to return to declare his love. And she laughed, said, *Is that what you tell all the girls?*—but knew at once from the fall of his face that he was telling his truth. She, five years or more into a dreary engagement, saw herself through his eyes and was immediately gone in her mind from the Nebraska family farm. After less than a year of ardent letters, she left to join him, returning only rarely for visits.

In our young years the romance of her story never faded. It is only now, with both lovers dead, that I find myself trying to reconstruct the story she didn't tell us: how she managed over fifty years to build her life with this kind of man—one who passively, doggedly held on to an adolescent crush for ten years, who never doubted that his loved one would understand his tardy, surprising return.

MOM'S SUMMER PEACHES

She knew how to pour them at the right pace. Slippery
        as goldfish, they slid into place, their shiny outsides
        facing outward, pressed into the jars' glass.

Peaches dominated her summers:
        waiting for Colorado Elbertas—those from
        California or Washington would not do.

She couldn't wait too long or the fruit was overripe.
        But early prices were too high. I hid my anxiety.
        Would she miss the perfect peaches this year?

Somehow she could always time it, or give up
        just before it was too late, complaining,
        paying the price for what she wanted.

They appeared in bowls at lunchtime
        and in Christmas fruit soup. Canned perfectly
        they were sweet and crisp tender.

She sneered at commercially canned cling peaches,
        called them slimy. Her summer obsession
        saved us from such inferior fare.

YOUR MOTHER'S HOME
(Namibia, Africa)

... for Esther Wanamene

You spread a quilt for us on sand below a solitary tree.
        Its leathery leaves rattle in midday breeze.

Once we've stretched out on the quilt, you carry from the
        house a white plastic chair for Anna, your sister.

Anna sits down. Her crisp secretary's dress
        crumples. She becomes
        youngest daughter, home at last.

The afternoon passes
        while sisters and cousins, neighbors and you
        take turns combing Anna's scalp.

They speak in Oshindonga while patiently
        straightening the tangles in her matted hair.

Sometimes you translate what they say;
        mostly you do not.

Like the light breeze, words that are just soothing
        sounds to me stroke my arms and face.

TIME

When I change my clock for Daylight Savings
I'm reminded—time is simply a human creation.

The truth is—there's never enough time
except, maybe, in childhood.

In their work geologists don't worry about days, decades,
or centuries. They explore eons.

Each year wild daisies open their blooms around
the same date, regardless of spring temperature.

Franz Wright reminds us, *Every star in the sky may be
nothing but light that still reaches your eyes* . . .

Humans spend lifetimes trying to modify natural cycles.
Animals survive by depending on theirs.

At a young age I discovered that
minutes, even hours, disappear easily into a book.

Terry Tempest Williams says about silence
. . . that is time you are hearing.

Regularly I recall the shock of my father's unexpected
death, but I can never remember how long ago he died.

How can we ever
imagine our own absence?

According to James Wright,
It's possible . . . to live forever in a split second.

During long winters I fear spring may never come. Then, from
under snowdrifts, snowdrop blossoms emerge, fully formed.

LATELY I'VE BEEN LOSING JEWELRY

First it was my father's wedding ring and then
it was just one earring of the pair I'd given
my mother, chosen because they shimmered
and swayed—moved as she moved. I don't know
how long they need to be gone before I decide
they are permanently lost. Till then I must
fight the urge to hunt for them constantly.

I wish I were part of a tradition that taught me the ring
was taken for my father to wear in another world,
that my mother has her favorite earring now—

but I believe our stories of meaning seep into our bones
from the moment of our birth. To borrow another's
tale is like donning a prosthesis after amputation—

you can walk on it, but
your blood does not flow through it.

What will we do with

everything that has been given us?

—Naomi Shihab Nye

EL SALVADOR VISIT, 1987

High stone walls topped with barbed wire
surround mansions of the wealthy.

Fires shoot up from garbage cans, lighting
faces of indistinct shadows.

We visit a village where all men are gone
except the old.

Outside McDonald's in San Salvador—
a guard with a machine gun.

We walk casually in pairs to meetings with
activists. We hope we won't endanger our hosts.

Outside of town, villagers take us
to the maize field where men were shot.

Speeding white vans with darkened windows
raise fears of disappearance.

Three human rights investigators—
two already dead; we meet the third.

Senators wearing black suits
deny the history of massacres.

At the beach no one seems to notice
the gray body near water's edge.

I say these things to remember . . .

CHICAGO BACK PORCH, 1951

If we duck down, we sisters are invisible.

Matching cotton skirts draped over granite gray boards,
we draw and cut,
eat peanut butter picnic sandwiches.

Through railing slats, slender slices of alley and yards:

identical yellow patches of parched grass,
huddled conversations over a hedge,
solitary walkers to the El.

Beneath that hedge far below, grow violets only I can find.

ON MY WAY TO ART CLASS AT AGE 9

—inspired by Marc Chagall's
THE PRAYING JEW, 1923,
Art Institute of Chicago

Heading again
to disappointment—
again my colors would be flat,
no life would leap from paper.

Suddenly stopped,
not knowing why,
I faced a rabbi's portrait.
Not much to see—black,
stark black sinking away from
white prayer shawl, aging beard,
warmer shadowed skin.
No clear color distracted.
Angular, awkward hands
lay in wait.
From within—
a phosphorescent glow.

His eyes urged me on,
sent me on my way.
Somehow now
I could continue on.

I told myself—
open your eyes,
use what you see,
what you know,
bring forth only
what you are.

EARLY MARRIAGE—
WEST VIRGINIA, 1968

The other nurses called them brambles:
prickly creepers climbing the rock face.
Stopping the car I gathered
blackberries to make an offering
for you—crystal jelly,
all seeds strained out through a tea towel.
Patients warned me later, *You better
watch out for copperheads on them cliffs.*

You came home from hospital duty,
tired and distracted,
spread my ambrosia thickly, and said,
I'd rather have Welch's.

———

To home visits I drove
on a dry creek bed overhung
with branches and vines.
It ended at a sagging porch,
vacant as the family processed a pig,
newly slaughtered, on the kitchen table.
Drawing me in near the carcass,
folks spoke their maladies: *blind staggers,
drizzlin' shits, a head gatherin'*
that went away with *white lightnin'*.

And you walked home from your shift
in the emergency room
with your own stories: a man impaled
through the chest with a telephone pole,
a woman with a neck goiter the size
of a cantaloupe; a child
whose *smilin' mighty Jesus*

was spinal meningitis.
We talked in the dark before you fell asleep,
feeling like Lewis and Clark.

———

Perched on the steepest hill in town,
our house was two stories high on the street,
four stories high in the back.
The gleaming Monongahela River
filled the winding valley bottom far below.

Years later my mother told us,
There was a hole in the bathroom wall.
I worried about rats.
We were surprised.
We couldn't remember a hole.

TEENAGED GIRL

. . . to my student

You are a window leaning up against a tree,
a door lying at the bottom of a ravine.
You are somewhere between liquid and solid—
slowly slipping from my grasp.

You are buffed, tweezed, shaved, powdered,
penciled in, and tinted. You paint yourself
into a corner, and even when the paint is dry,
refuse to walk out.

You seek out high places unprotected
while I stand below, barely able to watch.
I strain to read the direction signs you follow,
but they are in a language I no longer know.

DAUGHTERS WITH DISABILITIES

I can't write about

>your lurching gait, awkward, unbalanced;
>the miracle: you rarely fall;
>the work it takes for you to talk, processing
>what to say and how to form it.

I can't write about

>how I used to watch other families
>wondering if life was
>as easy for them as it appeared.

I can't write about

>the way I become invisible when I am with you
>as strangers avert their eyes or stare unblinking
>as if we can't see them gawk.

I can't write about

>how unexpected pain returns when friends
>tell of children's weddings, achievements,
>of grandchildren—pain as raw and briny
>as at diagnosis, but momentary.

I can't write about

>my disappointment in others
>and myself when we presume we know
>what you can and cannot do.

I can't write about

>your vulnerable walking in the world, unique,
>oblivious to my fears for you.

THAT DAY

The day our infant's doctor
called you to the phone
during work hours
out of your new responsibilities
still so overwhelming,
called you when you could only
half attend to what he was saying
because your ICU team
was making rounds without you,
called you to say
that your child who'd just
left his office with me your wife
(that child your only)
was to spend the rest of her life
with significant but unexplained
disabilities;   and you tell me
now forty years later
how it felt to be called that way
to that news, to receive it
alone, apart from us,
and be unable to do anything but
call me and return to work.

and you are still angry.

AFTER FIRST DIAGNOSIS

May it float underwater,
    may it stay
    submerged—
this news, this loss.

Then maybe
    I can immerse myself
    in my hopes,
never need to emerge.

Below
    edges are softened
    outlines unclear.
In dappled shade
    there is even
    a chance
it has not
    happened at all.

ANXIETY

In the midst of northern cold, I lose my ability to
stay hopeful. It shrivels in washed-out light.

Outside, neighborhood children play boisterously.
Are they unpracticed in the art of worry?

Wandering Israelites were told to consume at once
the manna God sent them—or it would rot.

It doesn't take much for my anxiety to rise up
like sucker shoots from crabapple tree roots.

It's always when I'm upset about something
that I make a mistake in following a recipe.

We cannot avoid spreading our shadows
unknowingly, unwillingly.

Jane Kenyon wrote, *If it's darkness we're having,
let it be extravagant.*

Anything can happen. Someday
my skull could be a trophy mounted on a spear.

The wood stork holds out her wings to dry them.
She makes herself completely vulnerable to predators.

I want to be clumped together like bread dough—
kneaded, turned, punched, made ready to rise.

RIDER

One of us would prepare you,
seat you on the trike
at the top of the long hill.

The slope was perfect.
You needed only to lift your feet
and you started to roll.

By the time you passed our driveway
you were moving fast enough
that you started to squeal.

The slope was perfect.
If you got going too fast
for your four-year-old comfort
you could drag your toes
and slow yourself down
to a gradual stop.

For those summer months
before we moved away
we kept buying new shoes
whenever the toes
wore completely through.

MAYO CONSULTATION

Not many memories from those days . . .

pushing and carrying a one-year-old,
praying tests won't be painful,
thankful when sedation is prescribed.

Just us two, mother and baby.
Older sister needs Daddy's care.

At day's end a phone call from home.
News in two voices:
soothing adult and eager eight-year-old.

But I remember that bouquet . . .

the only light in a shadowed hotel room.
Extravagant blossoms, yellow, white, red,
offered themselves as on an altar, waiting.

SWIMMING LESSON

...after second diagnosis

Forget that you
    can look through water.
It will hold you.

Forget how your foot
    cleaves it as you step in.
It will carry you.

Forget that each skin molecule
    is caressed by a water molecule
that each of your cells
    is filled with water.

You were born
    in a gush of water.
It will not dissolve you.

Whoever loves for years

    hasn't lived in vain.

        —Rolf Jacobsen

IN THE BEGINNING

You walked home
through a fog-bound park
at 3 AM after
our eager explorations
on my threadbare couch.
You followed streetlight glow
till suddenly aware—
just outside those luminous circles
a lurking amorphous shape
    shrouded in mist
    stealthy
    staying close
    moving only when you moved.

Later you recounted to me
with relief
how that figure slid off
into the gloom;
and we marveled together
at our good fortune,
proof in our developing minds
that we were lucky:
we'd escaped catastrophe.

We were so young.

ONIONS

I bought them
when money was tight—
onions, more than I needed.

Their glossy yet
papery skins
taut, golden. They were
available, affordable.
But they looked to me
an investment: currency
that could be spent
gradually, and, if kept well,
would seldom spoil.

I even thought some could
be planted to produce
a renewed crop.

As our new life together emerged
those onions added to
our unremarkable meals.

Their subtle flavor alerted us,
if we paid attention,
to what we needed to do
despite our youth,
our struggles and haste,
even our conflicts:

that is, seek out,
notice, and hold onto
what was easy to overlook
but always available:
each other.

MARRIAGE

     I

There is the official story.
Even we
have admired its shiny,
impenetrable veneer.

     II

I was taught
I should pour myself
into you. But you
don't want to be
force-fed like grass,
drenched
with fertilizer—don't
want to end the season
congested and sluggish,
unnaturally green
from my ministrations.

     III

Our argument, abandoned,
remains there as if we've
thrown a tablecloth over
an already set table.

     IV

We endured
grief storms
which blew us
to our separate
wailing walls. With time
and seeing the world
we've learned

the small scale
of our suffering. But
there is no size to pain.

V

We do not
tend a garden plot
carefully planned—
no black plastic
to block weed seeds,
just soil
open to the sky.

ALL ENTANGLED

Ice has no memory of water. In deep winter
it can't imagine ever being water again.

Albert Camus claimed, *We all carry within us
our places of exile, our crimes and our ravages.*

Technicians tell us
nothing can ever be completely deleted from a computer.

Some days the world is reversed.
The sun shines from beneath a fog bank.

Every piece of flotsam, tide-tossed,
reappears eventually. Nothing is wasted.

Analyzing Antarctica's ice layers, scientists can describe
the earth's climate patterns over past centuries.

Each spring cinnamon stick ferns appear overnight.
They grow to three feet tall within a few days.

Jane Kenyon wrote, . . . *my disordered soul
thirsts after something it cannot name.*

In June I found ice chunks
in the middle of my warming compost pile.

RELEASE

Jealousy escapes—darkens and spreads
like tea seeping into hot water,
bubbles out in a rush of wild stories; swells,
then overflows—a river reaching flood stage.

I've tried sandbagging: piled those bags high.
It never works. I must
dive in and ride the torrent—whirl in eddies
with random debris, spin past the riverbank—
film footage projected large. I must
shout my rage, my fear over roar of rapids,
use all my strength to cling to a slippery log.

Battered, spent,
tossed up on a littered shore,
I press outstretched fingers in toward my heart,
clutch its rise and fall.

EQUIPMENT

Rachel's Quad Canes

Small children always stared.
They must have seemed strange,
even threatening—those heavy metal canes
branched into four small feet,
each capped with a gray rubber tip.
After years of crawling, of holding a parent's hand,
she needed only hours of practice
to learn to take off
across open space, alone. It didn't seem long
till we stood at the sideline
as she ran race laps around a cinder oval.
Her feet churned as those canes
trailed off behind her   floating.

Beth's Stroller

She rode in her jumbo stroller,
stainless steel,
with a heavy-duty nylon seat
roomy and sturdy enough for
a five-year-old.
She rode like a monarch,
up high—surveying all around her.
Because she was small for her age
and the stroller large,
the scale seemed right.
We drew second glances
only occasionally.

FINDING EQUILIBRIUM

We could be
dragging
our only possessions
along an uphill path
as we watch
the horizon
for a cloud of dust
raised by our pursuers.

We could be
applying
pressure
to a spurting wound,
knowing,
as red soaks
through all compresses,
that life can run out.

But we are
holding
the hands
of this hip-high girl
who cannot walk
on her own,
who laughs up at us
in the joy of movement.

HOPE

My breath lies to me.
It tells me it can go on forever.

Daniel Berrigan said, . . . *the more serious the work to be done
the less one will see of the outcome.*

My daughter, Rachel, has disabilities that frustrate her.
She first hoped they would disappear completely.

Lucille Clifton wrote, *We think there's supposed to be
perfection, as if we understood even what perfection was.*

Viktor Frankl survived Nazi death camps. He reported that
prisoners with a vision for the future were those who survived.

Rachel's frustrations diminished
when she began to draw and paint.

―

Berrigan stated, . . . *the good is to be done
because it is good, not because it goes somewhere.*

I'm not sure all martyrs have hope.
If not, to what do they cling?

How old was I when I first understood
the sky is blue behind a gray wall of clouds?

In Rachel's painting, stars in a night sky are reflected
on dark blue water reaching for the far horizon.

Shortly before his death Frankl wrote,
Meaning is something to discover rather than to invent.

The sound of ocean tides
is in the water that washes my hands.

1982

...to Rachel

You flew from our home.
The beginning was not graceful or effortless.
No sailboat, cloud start.
You didn't know you had the design to glide:
      the perfect, efficient frame.
You felt the fear of escape, not its opportunities;
the risks, not the freedom.

Something changed and allowed you to trust,
to trust your buoyant self.
Now you are flying without strain.
Your pleasure as you glide is contagious: a wondrous
      thing to watch.
You have discovered your skill. There will be times of
      frenzied flapping again;
but now you know you are built to fly.

MOTHERHOOD

I was
    never confident
I could calm you.

Each time
you started
I wondered
    if you would
cry forever.
But I digress.
In a few minutes
I will call you.
I will hear
    your firm voice.
We will
make our plans.
I know
the kind of day
it will be.
I will work hard
to be a
    good listener,
not
    give advice
    or criticize,
and I will
hold back
    grateful tears.

WHEN RACHEL TURNED FORTY

... after Joyce Sutphen's "When You Were One"

When Rachel turned forty I had to
let her out from under surveillance.
For if I looked at her a long moment
she started to think I was judging her
or planning how to help. She seemed to
need nothing from me, she'd quietly

sidled out of reach. Suddenly
there were voices within her which I
had not heard, and there were
doors she walked through daily which I
had never opened. In her space
she had memorized hidden
corners that were invisible to me.

Once I'd assumed I would always
know her every move, but now
there was surprise each moment
I spent with her—as when, at forty,
she said, *Mom, I'll take care of you.*

STILL

    ... to Beth

The forecast
is for a winter storm.

My first thought
is how
your imbalance
makes it
difficult for you
to walk
on slippery sidewalks,
how your quad canes
sink into snow drifts,
making those supports
you lean on
unreliable.

You live
three hours away now.
There is nothing
I can do to protect you.

But still
you are
my first thought
when the forecast
is for a winter storm.

In a dark time

    the eye begins to see.

        —Theodore Roethke

LONG AFTER THE FUNERAL

...to another Mother

In gray early light
I guide my car along neighborhood streets
my way slowed
by an ambling yellow school bus.

Behind flashing red lights
I watch each pick-up: a preschool child
urged aboard by a patient mother—
last-minute words from the curb
a final parting wave.

Each stop a different pair—
different jackets and hats
       different colors and shapes.
But every time the same mother's face—
      gentle affection mixed with
      calm pride.

And I'm back at my young daughter's side
making quiet morning conversation.
We clutch ourselves in chill and dark,
prepare for the day's separation.

For the first time
since I heard the news of
your young daughter's murder, finally
I'm able to weep.

MOUNT ST. HELENS

Mountain slab rock
melted and boiled
over core fire exposed
when tectonic plates shifted
hundreds of miles away.

Battle ranks
of ancient trees
snapped—flattened
by the water blast
of magma-melted
glacial ice. Dun gray
cinders exploded
upward, trumping
the sun, piled up
speck on speck
till tree and rock
vanished beneath
a leaden blanket.

Only those
who fled survived—
no chance for a win
in the massive game
of rock-paper-scissors
played out here.

Treading ash this day
we study eruptions
of fir seedlings, flows
of elk on a moon landscape.

Survivors say May 18, 1980,
dawned a perfect morning.
So did today.

YOUR VOICE

> ... for Timo Rova, smokejumper, and
> the Holden Village community

You
told me
you crouched on
the other side
of the ridge, never
knowing when a wind shift
would bring flames over on top
of you. You said it so calmly—
flatly. But I saw charcoal matchsticks
fifty feet tall, skeleton groves draped on
mountainsides, smoke hanging in our valley
forty miles away; noticed with fear
the frank capriciousness of one
green slope, one black. Maybe it
was discipline I heard
buried in your voice
pounded in by
work, maybe
something
else.

DURING WAR IN AFGHANISTAN

At dawn the robin appeared
in the yew bush outside our window,
her nest wedged between three twigs.

How does she sit so long?

If only she'd leave so we can
see if there's down or chick inside.

There are beaks in the shadow.

Open mouths poke up urgently
out beyond the brim.

When will they fly?

This morning the nest is rent and tipped.
Only one neck still cranes.
On the ground below a tiny leg bone.

Now she's there only briefly.
The small head is quiet.
Then both are gone.

THE ZOO

Training Manual: *Refrain from anything that might not be good for the animals*

The zoo, near Buchenwald's only entrance,
outside its electrified fence, contained
four brown bears, five monkeys, an eagle.
The animals' enclosure faced an open Appelplatz. There
prisoners assembled twice a day
sometimes standing for hours.

It's official history . . . children of SS personnel
fed meat to the bears
in sight of prisoners.
Surviving inmates remember . . . prisoners
were fed to the bears by SS personnel,
bones picked clean by the eagle.

The zoo sat yards from
a crematorium inside the fence. There
bodies were taken after inmates died from
exhaustion, starvation, illness, strangulation,
shooting, or torture. Using mechanized equipment
fellow inmates loaded them into ovens.

Workers died quickly in that job.
Bodies routinely piled up outside the crematorium.
Residents of nearby Weimar received invitations
to visit the zoo, wander through its surrounding park.
A training manual for Buchenwald personnel stated
the zoo was created
for the enjoyment of SS guards and their families.

MY WORK

I keep track of the comings and goings of people.
My work is very simple. I write down and retain
the information that others give me.

When I started here they came in every day
with two lists of names to alphabetize.
First I added the names of those who had just come.
Then I crossed out the names of those who were gone.

Now the task is easier, but not as challenging.
We have instituted a number system. Numbers
are faster to find and take less space in the books.

I didn't agree with the change to numbers because
I thought they would be easy to transpose. But now
I realize that the volume of people coming and going
makes this change to numbers essential.

I tell myself, *I go home every night to my family.
My job isn't my whole life. If accuracy
doesn't matter to them, why should it to me?*

I'm proud I don't bring my work home with me.
I only think about work when,
from my balcony, I see and smell the smoke
coming from tall smokestacks on the other side of town.

—Poland, 1944

CERTAINTY

According to Rilke,
We have enough correct fools.

Don't we all love to make order out of chaos?
We're willing to do great damage to create order.

After seventy years the German government revealed a huge
storehouse with millions of Third Reich detention and execution files.

I find it most challenging to distinguish between
the intolerable and the unforgivable.

Forgiveness is a puzzle. It's what all world religions command, yet
it seems an unnatural task for humans.

Leaning into gale wind, I pace a frigid beach. Lake Superior
tosses up for me her iridescent ice floes.

Unquestioned beliefs made the Inquisition and Holocaust possible.
Doubt is more complicated, more subtle, even foolish.

I'm disturbed by gene research findings reported in THE NEW YORK TIMES
that raise questions about how much control we have over who we are.

In 1939 theologian Dietrich Bonhoeffer, eventual martyr, returned to Germany
from safety in the US. Reinhold Niebuhr questioned his mental health.

Mary Oliver wrote, *Let me keep my distance, always, from those
who think they have the answers.*

In her forties, the woman who had been horribly abused by her father
decided she would be free only if she spoke to him before he died.

Have you noticed—when daylight melts away ice glazing
the lakeshore, all rock cores are revealed, intact?

IN PRAISE OF FOG

The sky is the pearl lining of a clam shell,
the sun, a pale haloed glow.

There's kinship among shadows.
They sway like underwater plants.

A beaded curtain parts to reveal
one object at a time—glistening
and inordinately bright—
a tuft of grass, a stone, a cattail.

Each minute the last minute ...

—Denise Levertov

AGING

I clench my fingers, try to grasp water.
The tighter I clutch, the faster it slips away.

THE NEW YORK TIMES carried a headline:
Aging: Disease or Business Opportunity?

My sister and I emptied mother's apartment before her final move.
We sent off to the dump many possessions she prized.

During cadaver dissection in biology lab, students focused on
unique damages to a body: scars, a tumor, an artificial hip.

In John Banville's novel THE SEA, an elderly narrator says,
I have been elbowed aside by a parody of myself.

Aging is a form of oxidation.
The same general process occurs when iron rusts or fire burns.

I have long read obituaries. They change as I grow older.
Now I take inordinate comfort from those for the very elderly.

———

As I age, I notice my diminished energy. I'm not able to
help my daughters as much as I once did.

When I consider the universe—its far galaxies, its antiquity,
I'm reminded: I am not needed.

Charles Simic wrote of the natural reaction to thoughts of dying, *They held on to
a small hope that they would turn out to be exceptions to the rule.*

My daughters talk casually about my death. I'm gratified
they seem more comfortable with this eventuality than I am.

I wonder if what I cannot describe, what I cannot control,
is what will remain after I die.

In her book NINE GATES Jane Hirshfield advises,
Abandon all order and safety.

Looking back on my life, it seems the wake of a boat.
It flattens out even as I watch.

THE OLD WOMAN

She knows herself to be
as weightless and unrelenting
as dust.
The air barely moves.

She looks out again
into empty windows.
She's lived across from them
as long as she can remember.

She can only imagine death will be
another sloppy, confusing birth,
this time
into a place of deep stillness.

She considers that she
must wait to be used up.
Sunrise, unimpeded,
bounces between the windows.

She can only imagine death will be
another sloppy, confusing birth,
this time
into a place where she will be
empty, prepared to fill with light.

HER PHOTO

...for Robert

To live fully is to live with
an awareness of the rumble of terror
that underlies everything.
             —Ernest Becker

I barely knew her—a neighbor. Yet
I keep her photo nearby, the photo from
her newspaper obituary. Her face
looks back at me, vaguely familiar.
Each time I pull it out of my journal
I tell myself gently,
I will never see her again;
and each time, I remind myself patiently—
even this loss sends the rumble of terror
reverberating through me. I cannot
let myself contemplate fully
the earthquake of losing you.

QUILTS

She made them by hand with tiny, even stitches which wandered just enough that you knew it was sewn with simple needle and thread. She'd learned from her mother who'd also quilted, who used white cloth with one color at a time—lavender or chambray blue—always arranged into crisp geometric designs. My mother used patterns like sunbonnet girls, a crazy quilt, an intricately embroidered picture of the Nebraska farm where she was born. She used fabrics left from our home ec projects—aprons, skirts, dresses—cut out her shapes from their busy designs. Her quilts were like her clothes, colorful ones she wore even into her nineties. Once she made a satin quilt scattered with butterflies, all yellow and lavender.

Before she died in California, far from Dad's grave, she gave us instructions to cremate her—*easier to carry me back and bury my ashes with him*, she said. Her choice didn't bother me then. Today I dust off and refold her quilts. They've spent years in a closet. If only I'd been there, been able to wrap up her lifeless body in one of them.

ONE WORD

Mother, I asked you over the phone
how you were.
You said, "Almost."
Almost? Of course;
but it took your cloudy
ninety-five-year-old brain
to uncover that for me.

Almost. Almost on time. Almost done.
Almost able to say what's on my mind.
Almost alive. Almost dead.
Almost loving.

I've been grieving the loss
of your voice, of your mind.
It's been easier to turn away.
Now I'll try to pay attention.

IF I LOSE MY MEMORY

I'd walk out over the grass
in floppy terry cloth slippers
and find the frost-cleared plot.

I'd pull the volunteer weeds,
feel their reluctant release
from their underground hold,
draw the metal claw through
the outer crust and watch
the clods rotate after the cut,
rake through the chunks with
fingers warmed by heat
radiating from sunbaked soil.

It would be automatic for me
to find some dried brown seeds,
drill some holes, and drop them in.

If I lose my memory I might not
return to water or weed,
but it rarely matters.

Given time I would find
the arching bean sprouts,
the wispy carrot fronds;
and not knowing
the part I'd played, my surprise
would begin to approach
the wonder that is
appropriate.

THIS FACE

In sleep your face is
as flat and immobile
as an unruffled pool.

At some time in the night
it may have been
stirred by a passing dream.
Your mouth may even have
uttered a word.

But now in early light
you lie here
placid,
your features—anyone's.

I want to wake you,
watch your eyes fill
with dark glowing light
as they turn to
focus on me.

I need to be reassured.

For this face,
distant and unperturbed,
will someday
never more return to me.

AT THE FUNERAL

. . . for my widowed friend

She opens and closes her lips slowly
like a tropical fish
flutters her tissue like a chiffon fin.

With a sideways nod of her head
      and a swallow
she raises her eyes reluctantly to the pulpit.

Muffled words float around her.

beloved husband

                                                  death
                  darkness

never-failing love

                            child of God

      loss

              consolation

                                separation

When the murmur stops, she rises,
      wobbling, and begins
her swim against the weight of water.

THE PAST

Wood smoke roils over the ridge, dips into the valley,
then lifts and vanishes into flat white sky.

Returning to the street where I lived during grade school,
I had my picture taken in front of the wrong house.

Are the most significant events of my life
those I can't remember?

One of my recollections glows with its own mystery.
Why can't I recall what makes it so powerful?

Each day is the anniversary of
some event which will not recur.

The first frost stiffens blades of grass.
They look the same; but wind can no longer move them.

Neuroscience research has demonstrated:
we make changes in our memories throughout our lives.

Susan Rich asked,
Is memory a chain of alibis?

Grieving her husband, my cousin says her favorite photo
of him soothes her one day, causes her pain the next.

Could it be that the sum of our experiences
is simply preparation for the leaving of life?

Undulating ridges in snow's crust
are all that remain of the winter wind.

AUTUMN GARDEN

Behold the sturdy brussels sprout
upright against October wind,

carrot fronds as yet unfrozen
signal orange roots—sweet still,

withered pea vines—whitened, chalky—
rattling reminders of fresh-picked flavor,

emptied weed seed pods mark
where next year's crop is planted.

Behold! We may not be temporary.

Those who are willing to be vulnerable

move among mysteries.

—Theodore Roethke

RAINY MORNING

I remember...
it was natural to seek explanations.
I craved them. Questions from others sought them.

When Rachel and Beth were old enough, they asked
their own questions. The responses, then, always partial:

*Since both sisters are similar
we can only guess it's a recessive, inherited condition.*

*Since their condition is so rare, it probably
would not show up in the next generation.*

Now there are more sophisticated tests available—
brain scans, genetic analyses.

Maybe now some explanation could be concocted
from new data, from a fresh review of symptoms.

Driven by northeast wind, rain lashes my window.
I can't explain the movement of weather fronts,
discuss the dynamics of water condensation.

I watch drops roll down the pane,
trace my fingertip through misted surface.

THAT MOMENT

That precise moment of dawn
when light has not yet
left the backlit clouds to come
to shine on each object here,

when light suffuses the whole
expansive backdrop of sky
leaving us bereft:

that is the moment
when we can see, if we look,
every discrete detail of the shape
of these trees in crisp relief before us,
their surfaces drained of color,
their silhouettes solid and defined.

TO MY ADULT DAUGHTER

You go to church weekly
with a prewritten check
far exceeding a tithe
of your sub-minimum wage.

You read your Bible
every day and always
remind me when it's time
to reorder your reading guide.

You recount in detail
the main points
of a sermon
you particularly enjoyed.

You still carry in your Bible
the index cards
your grandmother sent you,
Bible verses
about God's care and love,
verses she'd carried herself
and added to after
your grandfather's death.

You discuss dispassionately
the fact I'll die some day
without saying
what you believe happens next.

You don't raise
the questions I do.

CLUES

Birch trees shimmer behind the spruces.
They barely flash their ghostly skins.

The woman who has Alzheimer's
answers only in echoes.

When we were children, the corner house glowed
with mystery. We made up stories about it incessantly.

My father left his solitary study and entered the pulpit.
There he preached his message ruthlessly.

I always thought if I could decipher words from voices
coming through our walls, maybe they'd offer an answer.

Theodore Roethke wrote, *I fear those shadows most
that start from my own feet.*

Walking at night along city streets
I search for a silhouette in a distant lighted window.

As my friend described her childhood traumas,
any easy familiarity I'd had with her dissolved.

Fearing the future, most of us rush to choose
a diminished life. Doing so, we must miss so much.

I think now
my father's message was hidden in his silence.

According to Mary Oliver, *There are so many stories
more beautiful than answers.*

Under the dock where I stand, shadows glide back
and forth, reveal the lake's breathing.

LIGHTING CANDLES ON ALL SAINTS' DAY

Some start naturally, blend easily
into the flame of a tall Christ candle; but
when pulled away, struggle to sustain their light.

Some crackle loudly as they ignite—announcing
their achievement. But the persistence
of radiance is not guaranteed.

There are those who need extra care at first—
straighten their wicks,
keep longer contact with the fire.

Only a few grasp the fire
as their own and glow
nearly as steadily as the source.

One taper will not ignite. The wait
stretches on. Must this one be discarded?
Slowly, a fragile flame appears.

The sand tray is full. Light
flares up resplendent, dances out
into dark vast space.

UNEXPECTED WONDER

I can imagine how it started: unexpected wonder followed by the desire to preserve it. A meteorologist before weather satellites, my father photographed clouds. Everyone told him he was lucky to have "a good job" during the Depression; but he craved a Divine Call. Climbing up on the airport roof to pull in weather balloons, he brought along his camera and tripod. Soon he and my mother were there on the weekends when conditions were right for specific cloud formations. He captured a perfect cumulonimbus cloud set in a pre-storm sky. That image became the trademark for a marshmallow company. His picture of flat nimbostratus, gray and knobby, showed an example so average it appeared in ENCYCLOPEDIA AMERICANA as the visual definition of "cloud." But the rarest form he recorded was a nameless twisted wisp lying parallel to the horizon. Apparently unremarkable, it showed the inner workings of cloud building. Preserved on our parsonage wall, whenever Dad explained it, we marveled.

LIFE FORMS

I

Dry-eyed cirrus clouds
clasp the stratosphere—
sheer brittle ice wisps that disappear
while they slide past the sun.

II

Cumulonimbus clouds
glide proudly in their channels—
large ships pushed by a master wind.
When one unfurls
into an anvil thunderhead,
hurls down its rain, that cloud
lives on through the night,
hiding the moon, delaying the day.

III

Cumulostratus cloud blankets hug the earth,
sometimes so closely
they're torn by hilltops. Serviceable
and plain, they simply give up their rain.

MORNING GLORIES

Our first problem—
we started with seeds, not plants.
Then summer was unexpectedly cool.
Vines barely grew,
no buds developed till late in August.

Finally the first flower appeared,
fully open at dawn, a sunrise
of blue unclouded sky
blushing pink rays of light.

We won't welcome flower-laden vines.
Our harvest—single blossoms
each living a single day.
We rush to the patio daily,
celebrate each one. Devotion
is all we can offer till frost comes.

HAPPINESS

When I visited poor families in El Salvador,
I was surprised they seemed as content as I was.

Poet Jane Kenyon wrote, *there's no accounting for happiness,
or the way it turns up like a prodigal.*

Jesus didn't talk about happiness. "Blessed" is the most accurate translation
for the first word used in his Beatitudes in the Gospel of Luke.

When we first learned our daughter was disabled,
our fear was she wouldn't be able to lead a satisfying life.

In STUMBLING ON HAPPINESS, Daniel Gilbert claims research has shown
humans are ill equipped to predict what will make them happy.

―

I can't predict who among the elderly I know
will accept aging, illness, and death with equanimity. I am often surprised.

For many years psychotherapists tried to define the basic human drive.
Freud proposed sex; Adler proposed self-actualization; Frankl proposed meaning.

Once people who committed suicide were buried outside the churchyard
because they had committed a sin. Now they are diagnosed with an illness.

At times I experience intense joy. I believe it's a habit—not something I can create.
If I try to analyze the feeling, it disappears immediately.

Daniel Kahneman won the 2002 Nobel Prize in Economics for his development
of hedonic psychology, the study of what makes life pleasant or unpleasant.

―

Our daughter is miserable when she doesn't have a job. What matters most to her
is not the money she earns. She can be quite happy volunteering.

Pascal claimed all seek happiness, without exception. He said,
This is the motive of every action of every man, even of those who hang themselves.

I can't remember who said that the height of our joy
is usually commensurate with the depth of the sorrow we've experienced.

In explaining his theory Victor Frankl liked to quote Nietzsche:
He who has a why to live can bear almost any how.

A WALL STREET JOURNAL article analyzed happiness scores of the richest Americans.
Their scores were slightly higher than those of Swedes or Maasai tribesmen.

———

Jesus said his Father in heaven *makes the sun rise on the evil and on the good,
and sends rain on the righteous and on the unrighteous.*

After thirty-six years of caring for cancer patients, my husband is still amazed
there is more laughter in cancer clinic than in most other places.

Poet Beverly Rollwagen complains everyone wants her to be happy all the time;
but she says, *there is value in the thread of sadness in each person.*

I believe we are born with individual optimism thermostats.
Some people feel hope easily, while others rarely feel it.

We worked hard to remove barriers from our daughter's life, to make it easier for her.
Now that she's on her own, she seems to thrive when she deals with some challenge.

———

Recent research shows that brain chemicals cause depression; but families still
use code to describe a son's suicide: *his unsuccessful struggle with sadness.*

My mother loved her beautiful possessions: china, silver, jewelry, clothes.
I was surprised she let them go easily as she moved into smaller and smaller spaces.

Gilbert reports healthy people rated eighty-three illnesses as worse than death.
But people actually with these illnesses rarely take their own lives.

When I hear about a successful suicide I always want to know how.
My husband says he always wants to know why.

As I've grown older I've come to believe
that the fairy-tale ending *they lived happily ever after* is not a blessing.

ABOUT THE AUTHOR

ANN FLOREEN NIEDRINGHAUS began writing poetry after twenty years of marriage, raising two daughters who have disabilities, and pursuing a career as a registered nurse, social worker, nonprofit agency executive, and teacher. In her more than twenty years of writing since, her poems have appeared in numerous journals and anthologies and in her chapbooks, *Life Suspended* and *Parallel to the Horizon*.

Ann was born in Moline, Illinois, but her family quickly moved to Chicago. She is influenced by her early life experiences there and in New Jersey; Saskatchewan, Canada; South Dakota; Minnesota; West Virginia; and southern California. When she returned to Minnesota, she lived in Rochester and, for forty years, Duluth.

Her life in Duluth was full of her work; annual retreats to Holden Village; travel to Central America in the 1980s; providing a home for a student from Namibia, Africa; and her volunteer work, especially offering poetry writing workshops. Her favorite workshops were for inmates in the St. Louis County Jail.

Ann's writing has been shaped profoundly by her association with her writing group of over twenty years. Together they published two poetry anthologies of their work: *The Moon Rolls Out of Our Mouths* and *Bound Together: Like the Grasses*. *Bound Together* won the 2013 Northeastern Minnesota Book Award in poetry.

After retirement, Ann settled in Saint Paul with her husband, Robert, near her daughters, Rachel and Beth. *All Entangled* is her first full-length book.